NOVEMBER 28TH, 2015

12 MONTHS AFTER

ANTWAUNE FISHER

Antwaune Fisher
November 28th, 2015

Published by BooxAi
ISBN: 978-965-578-744-3

NOVEMBER 28TH, 2015

A glimpse into the worst year of a parent's life

2015 WAS the year that forever changed me, not only as a person but also as a man. I had spent four years out of prison and was in my third year at my job, which, at that time, I had never done in my forty-one years of living. I had re-established my relationships with family, friends, and, most importantly, my kids. My daughter and I were in a genuinely great place. My one and only son and I had also gotten to a great place once I stopped trying to make him into the son/man I wanted him to be. I began dealing with him as the man/son he was and that made it easier for us to communicate. After that, we were able to get to a genuine place; a place where we could talk. Being a dad that my kids could talk to at any time about anything was the most important thing for me because it allowed me to see how my kids needed me after prison. If I'm being honest, I truly had no clue how I would be useful to them since they'd been so well taken care of by their moms and their stepdads.

2015 was also the beginning of me wanting to be in a relationship. It was the first time since I'd been home that I felt like I was tired of just being out there. I wanted someone who was there for me. All of these *firsts* were happening to me at the same time. For a person like me who's a thinker by nature, naturally, all of these things had me thinking and looking at things differently. I guess another way you could put that is that I was growing up or maturing, and because of this, another 'first' was taking place for me. I wanted to get better at handling money to put myself in a position to buy a house. I felt like I was in a place where I needed to set up stability for myself so that I could be more of the man I felt I was becoming at the time. If I wanted forever, I had to put myself in a position to take care of it, and my fear became not wanting to be the reason it didn't work.

All of these 'firsts' had me in a great place mentally. I went to my TT to come up with a plan for me to start saving money to buy a house. I was beginning to see how I could still be there for my son since our relationship was getting stronger. I could feel my purpose starting to develop. After six years in prison, where I learned about myself, I was finally in a place mentally where I understood myself and what I wanted and didn't want. More importantly, I knew who I was as a man and who I wasn't, so confidence was at an all-time high. I felt for the first time that my being in prison wouldn't be a hindrance for me. My level of understanding when it came to dealing with people and whatever relationship we had was good. This was also a pivotal year for me as a man because I was beginning to see myself in the future, and that was something I'd never really done before. Due to my upbringing, I could enjoy the moments from day to day, which carried over into my adult years. Again, that changed when my kids were born, but looking or thinking years down the line still wasn't a thing for me until 2015. Like I said before, a lot of 'firsts' took place that year, all different, all life-changing.

Now imagine being in such a place physically, mentally, and even spiritually that you feel you can do anything you put your mind to, but all you can think of is how getting a house means more time, scratch that, unlimited time, with your kids. My son would stay with me, and my daughter would have a key. So she would be able to visit whenever she wanted. I was working the second shift at the time, so I thought of coming home one

Friday night, and both of my babies would be in my house when I got home after missing six years of their lives because I decided to be stupid. I couldn't have written a better script for a parent who, to say the least, had been a disappointment, considering how much I love my babies. The laughter, conversations, and all-around good times with my babies were heavy on my mind. I wasn't impatient, but I was very anxious. See, before prison, one of my favorite things to do was watch movies with my babies because, for that moment in time, I was not too bad of a dad in their eyes, and for me, that was like heaven on earth. With them now (at this time) being twenty-one years old, I was looking forward to a lot of laughter.

Imagine having that feeling for eleven months and twenty-seven days only to be told on the twenty-eighth day that your only son is dead.

YES! DEAD!

The day after Thanksgiving, I got a call from my son's mom, letting me know he had been in an accident. She told me what she knew, and I told her I was on my way to the hospital, where she and her husband were already. Before I get too far into November 28th, 2015, I want to explain again where I was mentally up until that day with a little more clarity. See, when I came home from prison, I had no expectations when it came to my relationships with family and, most importantly, my kids. I did, however, have a ton of fears due to the reality of my situation. I wasn't coming from a good thing; I got stupid and took myself off the streets away from my loved ones. They had every right to be upset and just different from me, especially my babies. To my amazement, I was not hit with either family or my babies. Being the type of person I am and knowing my loved ones the way I do, there was an understandable air of disappointment, which, to their credit, never really showed. The fact that my mom and aunt made sure I had what I needed when I got out to Texas, and my sister made sure I had a phone of my own that I didn't have to worry about, tells it all.

On top of that, my kids decided they would do spring break in Texas with me. My daughter already planned to be there since her cousin lived there, but my son asked to come there to see me, and his mom and stepdad made it happen. When he told me that he was coming, it was like seeing him in the hospital for the first time. I'm not sure how I found out my baby girl was coming to Texas, but I know how blessed I was/am to have kids who genuinely love their old man. Despite my shortcomings, I did my time in Texas, so when I was paroled, I paroled in Texas, then switched my parole to Michigan. That's important to know, too, because that means there was no direct communication between my kids and me for six years. So, for them to want to see me was big, especially during the spring break of their senior year. My daughter stayed with her cousins, which was for the best due to me getting money from my mom, and my Mexican friend was helping me get around because my son stayed with me. I'm broke with no transportation in Houston with my son, and he never complained. We ended up having a lot of conversations without any awkwardness. That, in a nutshell, was my first year out. I was released in March of 2011 but didn't move back to Benton Harbor for good till December of that year. By the time I got home for good, my mentality was in a good place because of my kids, so when 2015 hit and all of the 'firsts' took place, I felt like I was ready to take the next step in life with my kids, and hopefully with a woman in my life.

Now imagine having experienced all of that, as well as processing it and getting an understanding of what you now feel is a part of your purpose. Only to have that purpose taken away before you get a chance to fulfill it. Imagine learning about your relationship with God while in prison and getting that understanding of how He has moved in your life and how you've been messing up. Although I would find out years later what this was about, at the time, it didn't make sense to me to have me leave prison, thinking my purpose was to be a better father with a better presence in their lives. So you bless me to be able to make parole only to take my only son away from me. That, to me, is what made things so crazy for me. I was sure I understood why I went through what I'd gone through until that point in my life. One of the things I grew to understand while in prison was everything happens for a reason, and if you are honest with yourself about what you're experiencing, you can learn what that reason is and respond accordingly.

Now, all of that understanding and purpose gets blown out of the water when God decides it's time to call your only son home without giving you the chance to make it right or do better. Everything I felt he revealed was for nothing. All the understanding, all of the acceptance that I'd learned, everything, even blessing me with parole, seemed pointless. Believe it or not, it was a very real feeling for me. It was a question I asked out loud, knowing full well the love I have for my daughter and the rest of my family as well. Not to mention the fact that I loved being free; for me, at that moment, I no longer had a purpose, so what was the point of being out there?

The first question asked is, "What about your daughter?" because it is assumed that I'm not considering her when I say that, but nothing could be further from the truth. I am very realistic about my relationship with my baby. I know she loves me just like she knows I love her, but she also knows that the parents she can depend on are her mom and stepdad. As she grew older and our relationship grew, she realized what her dad's use was in her life, but at the time, she would have been OK hurting because of her love for me, but fine, nonetheless. It may have made our relationship different when I finally came home, but I believe we would have still had a relationship. As for my family, they all have their own families, so again, they may be hurt because they love me, but they would've been fine as well.

As a man, not having purpose was just the tip of the iceberg once my son was gone. I also lost confidence, motivation, and the ability to control my emotions. I felt like less of a man for being unable to protect my son. How he was taken doesn't matter. I was his dad! I was supposed to protect him! I brought him into this world in a foul way by having two women pregnant at the same time, but I couldn't provide for him consistently, nor could I protect him. NOW WHAT? Tell me again why I should be out here! Let me be perfectly clear about one thing: at no point and time did I ever contemplate suicide. Due to the realization that I had to accept the fact that I was a failure, I truly didn't care what happened to me, which is why it made more sense for me to finish my sentence in prison. But, since I was free, I just developed an 'I don't care' mentality. I didn't care if I ate, slept, worked, or talked to another living soul ever again. I was on a level of 'I don't care' that was so high. As things came to me, I learned every day that these were things I didn't care about either.

I was as confused as I had ever been!

I couldn't make simple decisions like where I wanted to sit down in the house; whether I wanted to sit up or lie down was something I had trouble trying to decide. If I got to sleep at all, I would sometimes wake up and could not catch my breath. All I could do in those moments was scream on my pillow and/or cry as hard as possible. I also experienced the loneliest loneliness during the first few months, like I had never felt before, which further led to my confusion since I didn't have him on a day-to-day basis. As an only child, I'd never felt alone until I went to prison, the second time being when my son was taken from me. I wish I could say I had an overwhelming feeling come over me that made me OK with God's decision to call him home, but I didn't! Instead, I wanted to know what possible reason He could have for this. WHY? Since this was His doing, I had to wait for him to tell me, and since I didn't care about anything, I planned to sit in one spot until he let me know what he could possibly be trying to teach me or open my eyes and make me aware. What could I have done that would make this make sense to God? I know some of the dos and don'ts when it comes to God, but I didn't care at this moment! I had questions, and I needed answers.

Don't get me wrong, I have friends who, to their credit, were the best at 'understanding' during that time. The thing about that, though, is I know the type of father they are; the last thing I want to do is put that on their mind or anyone else's mind, including my family. Who wants to be associated with that? Not to mention that they all had their relationship with my baby boy, especially my mom—his grandmother—they had to deal with. We could not be in each other's company for the next five to six months without tearing up. It was so intense we kind of stayed away from each other until we couldn't; we had to see each other!

If I'm being honest, having to go through something like this alone made it a thousand times worse for me. The loneliness pushed me to look for comfort wherever I could find it. Luckily, the only drug I have ever done or wanted to do was weed, and I'm not a drinker like that, so I had to sit there and do nothing or drive with no apparent destination. Those were the things I used to find comfort. I did use women for sex and company at times, but not having someone there that I had 'that connection' with who was there to comfort me, could be nothing more than a hug or just letting me know I wasn't alone, was one of the things that made it much harder to get through day to day. One of the first things that stood out to me was it seemed like I got more support in prison than I did with the loss of my baby. Because I was emotional, I had to be careful with the way I responded to those who felt like they were doing or saying something that would help.

Another reality I had to accept was that the individuals you believed would know you the best would deal with you based on what they knew. I quickly found out that what I thought people knew of me was not the same as what they thought. Learning that the ones close to you don't see you the way you think you've been portraying yourself your entire life is a tough pill to swallow. It also made it harder for them to help me, especially since this was also new territory for them. On top of all that, I learned something else when it comes to my relationship with my family. There has been a dynamic that I wasn't aware of due to my ignorance. Being raised by my mom, my grandma, and my auntie, I was allowed to figure things out for myself for the most part. Now, when I figure it out, depending on what it is, I move accordingly. What usually happens is I screw it up, go to them, and they just fix it. For the majority of my life, that was part of my comfort zone; whether it worked or not, as far as I was concerned—it worked for me. That is until it didn't!

On November 28th, 2015, I looked to my family for comfort, but all they wanted to do was fix me or make me feel better. The truth is that if you are dealing with something like this for the first time, you're not going to know what to do, but the love they have for me makes them want to do what they naturally do. That leads to the old tried and true tactics that everyone uses to attempt to make you feel better without actually paying attention to me, to see if what they are about to say or do is even applicable to me. From my perspective, it just seemed like they wanted to fix my situation, and this was not a 'fix it' sort of situation. The obvious remedy was therapy, but the problem for me with that and/or anything else at that moment was I wanted and felt I needed answers. I knew who caused the problem and why he claimed to do what he did, which was drive drunk to try and take his own life.

I needed the reason that God had for all the pain I was in, and I needed to understand why this had to happen at the time that it happened. What lesson could I possibly need after six years in prison? Most of what I had learned from my mistakes or losses before this I could use to make me a better person. How in God's name was this supposed to make me better? Is it even possible without that part of me? These were some of the immediate questions, as every day brought a new question that I needed answers to. Again, from my perspective, therapy was not going to answer any of those questions. As an only child, my cousins were my siblings, but by the time this took place, everyone had their own lives, so I was truly in a place where I had to figure this out on my own. It sucked more than anything I have ever done or has happened to me. The best friends, who at this point are family, were great at understanding while they watched their brother go through something they couldn't imagine going through.

My mom and I moved to Maryland when I was young, but I would always want to come back to Benton Harbor. As I got older, I would alternate between spending summers in Benton Harbor and going to school in Maryland. I always felt like Benton Harbor was my home, no matter where my mom and I lived. The level of comfort I feel in Benton Harbor is why it was and always will be home. That being said, I am now at the worst point in my life, in the place where I've always been able to find comfort, and now not only can I not find it, but I'm also alone. Loneliness, seeking comfort, extremely emotional, and learning that at the end of the day, *NO ONE* has to give a fuck about what you are going through. We can want someone to care; we can assume they should, but at the end of the day, they don't have to. It sucked to learn it at that moment, but I learned to understand it later. The more I accepted that the more I began to stay to myself but still looked for the love and comfort of a woman to take care of me emotionally. That wasn't the smartest thing to do because it puts you in a position to accept whoever will spend time with you at your lowest point. All these things naturally had me all over the place mentally, and I still needed answers.

Throughout all this time, I'm still checking my phone at the times my son would normally call or text. I'm trying to think of all the things in my day-to-day life that will be affected by the fact that my child is no longer here. I did have one cousin and one friend who offered their homes to me and let me vent or cry whenever I needed them, and they will never know how valuable that was to me. That's not to say no one else did or would've done the same thing, but those two were immediate. Those two people and my brothers had front-row seats to me being all over the place, literally and figuratively. I'm sure they wanted to tell me to "shut the hell up" many of the nights, but to their credit, they never did.

Doing anything at all became a chore as 2015 came to an end. After realizing the last time I saw my baby and the last time we talked, I just felt like the reason for this had to come to me quickly because I'm not sure how long I can live like this. I've always done factory work, but it was because mentally, I could look past the way they treat me, but now that I'm this new emotional person, I can't do that anymore. Had I been in a better place financially, maybe I wouldn't have had to go back to work so soon. But I wasn't, and I had to. An emotional man like me, in a place I feel I have to be, and I know they don't have to nor care to give a fuck about what I'm going through. That's not an ideal situation for me to succeed in. I was out of control emotionally, so I could overlook how they treated me day to day.

I later worked at a place during the start of the pandemic that told us we were essential because we made showers and bathtubs. That made us essential because you could die if you didn't take a bath or shower every two days. I am old enough to understand that if you tell someone something you don't believe but want them to believe, you must think of them a certain way, which is usually less than or expendable. Either way, it's not good. On top of that, due to me going to prison, anything that I feel I must do, which is an emotional thing or makes me feel like I had to be there physically and can't leave, made me feel like I was in prison. That feeling of not having control of what you can or can't do when you can or can't leave. I can't have that feeling in the free world, even when I'm on parole. Needless to say, I lost jobs due to this, which made loneliness even louder. It also made me care even less about what happens to me; as far as bills or anything of the sort. I truly couldn't care less about those things.

So, to recap: I am emotionally out of control, lonely, have no purpose, no confidence, no money, and am in search of comfort and understanding. I don't have a clue why all of this is going on. All of that occurred before Christmas. By the time the New Year rolled around, the loneliness was at an all-time high. That was what the actual first year after my son's death was about. I wanted to do anything to silence that loneliness. I am a man who reacts emotionally but did not realize at the time that combination can lead a person to overlook some things that are most likely things you wouldn't normally overlook. I was no different, especially since I, at the time, was looking for comfort, which I was also attaching to loneliness. Because of all those things running together, I would spend time with women for sex just to feel good for a moment. It was a feeling that didn't last long, and I'd usually feel worse for a while afterward, but as soon as that would wear off, I'd do it all over again. The problem with that was I knew I was tired of that and wanted someone who would be there for me, especially at that time.

While I may have wanted that, I was also realistic about my situation, which was not good enough to be the man I wanted to be for the rest of my life. From my perspective, if a woman was willing to deal with me, or any man for that matter when he was at the lowest/worst time in his life, it should say a lot about her as a person as well as a woman. Under normal circumstances, I would be able to make sure that I was seeing what I was seeing, and hearing what I was hearing. However, in this situation, my mental state was everything but normal, not to mention I was truly basing my decision on the fact that I was at my lowest. I'm also loudly insecure about myself as a man in general, so it's not going to happen despite me knowing it is a possibility. I also had to factor in where my age group of women were in life at the time, and I just became a black man with emotional issues.

One of the things that rang out to me was how men are treated when they are going through something. I felt no woman was going to want to deal with that, and the ones that would, we didn't work as anything more than friends due to the type of people we were. I would have conversations with women where I would try to explain how we didn't work, but it was never taken well or right. So when my son died, and I looked to those women for comfort, I could only get that physical feel-good for the moment cause I already knew we didn't work the way I needed us to work. Again, emotionally, I was out of control, so I responded to everything from an emotional place without applying any thought to it at all. For me, that's a lot in itself because, before Tae's death, I was a thinker by nature. I had to think things through until it made sense for me to do it. Even the dumb shit I did, I had to make it make sense to me minus the emotion, and I was able to do that.

After his death turned me into this new emotionally reactionary person, I wasn't able to do that. None of this made me feel good about my chances of having someone in my life to silence the loneliness. I'm also still waiting for the reason for taking my son in the first place, which can sometimes put me in a foul mood. All that being said, who would think a simple DM would lead me to think that what I felt was so unattainable to me?

It didn't really happen till closer to my second year when I contacted the woman who I felt was willing to deal with me. After I explained where I was mentally, I only began to feel because I wanted it so badly. To know a lot while getting to know someone during the worst time in your life will make you miss or overlook things about a person you shouldn't, especially when that loneliness gets louder every day. Things began to change because this woman was willing to spend time with me despite where I was in life at the time. I instantly began to feel like the loneliness was getting quieter and quieter. Obviously, I can say a lot about my getting into a relationship at that time and why I shouldn't have done that. But at the time of the relationship with this woman, my mind was solely focused on not being alone. I knew it couldn't just be anybody.

So imagine my surprise when I explained where I was mentally, emotionally, and financially, and this woman still wanted to spend time with me.

Now, from my perspective, I was truly doing my due diligence on getting to know her and making sure I was open about myself as well. I got to know her story, and that made it even easier to excuse the things I saw. The connection was there, but if I were able to take my emotions out of it, I would've been able to make a better decision when it came to getting involved with someone. I remember that at the time, I had no clue I wasn't making good decisions in general, let alone capable of choosing me forever. Again, from my perspective, I was thinking things through and was paying attention to the things being said and done by everyone. I was especially focused, at the time anyway, on the fact that a woman would deal with me at a time when I didn't even look like the man I am now, let alone the man I want to be for the woman in my life. Under normal circumstances, I wouldn't have put so much weight on one act like that, but at the time, in this day and age, that made me excuse or just flat-out overlooked things about this woman that just didn't work based on the type of people we were. Because the connection was real, there was a love there, but it wasn't sustainable. Honesty, the last thing I needed was to be in a relationship at that time because I didn't realize I literally and figuratively was all over the place. Instead of trying to find comfort in someone, I should have been trying to get an understanding of why that even happened. Thanks to the loudness of the loneliness, though, all I wanted was to quiet the loudness. Because of my reasoning for getting into a relationship, I put myself in something that was best built on a shaky foundation. Needless to say, I met and fell for a woman. In a lot of ways we worked, but in reality, we didn't work in a lot of very important ways. I can say now that I take full responsibility for even getting involved with someone for the wrong reason.

One of the things I knew before my son passed was that for

me to have a healthy relationship, I had to be with the woman because of her and nothing else. If I had any other reason or need that I was putting on her and the relationship, the minute that need or reason was no longer a thing that gets attention, things would typically begin to change for the worse in the relationship, which would eventually lead to the breakup. Ultimately, that's exactly what happened to me and my eventual marriage that ended after a three-year relationship – I shouldn't have ever gotten into it in the first place. That relationship started towards the end of what was the worst year of any parent's life.

Everything else I described was at the beginning of what was becoming the worst year of my life. Now, the middle consisted of me dealing with the day-to-day reality that I would never talk to my son or see him again. I thought about how he didn't get a chance to have any kids or get married. I have to deal with the fact that the day he died, he texted me for a ride, and I put him off because I was getting my radio put in my truck. I think he wanted a ride to the side of town I was already on. I told him I'd come to get him, but it would be a while. Who knew? The middle was filled with the belief that my failures as a man made all of this grief possible. Logical or not, it made sense to me, leading me to think things through from that perspective, creating more guilt that I can't do anything about. The theme of the middle, or should I say one of the themes, was GUILT.

Guilt was front and center because of my failures as a dad, regardless of why it was there. Losing my son made me replay all the ways I let him down and how I wouldn't have a chance to make that up. Another one of the lessons I learned after prison was the beauty of having a good relationship with your kids: you will always get a chance to right a wrong at some point in their life, as long as you are a part of their life. At the very least, you will have a chance to apologize as a parent. That's all you can do sometimes. Realizing how I let him down just by going to prison was guilt enough to last a lifetime. When you factor in the guilt I already had for having two kids at the same time and then not being ready or mature enough to take care of them without the help of my family, I was in a hell that I didn't see a way out of. I even felt guilty for thinking all of this because I felt as though I was making his death about me. I'm sure that's not a rational way to think about what I was feeling, but that is also what I was feeling. Knowing what to do was a chore, whether it was knowing how to feel or what to do from day to day or anything else for that matter. Knowing that my kids were and are a part of me, it's hard not to feel responsible for the loss. My kids are ingrained into who I am, which is why I can say I lost a part of me.

On top of all that, PARENTS ARE NOT SUPPOSED TO BURRY THEIR KIDS. That is not the circle of life, which is why, immediately after being told he was dead, I could hear my grandma say what she was saying when my uncle, her oldest, died, which was that *parents aren't supposed to bury their child*. For a while, I'd hear that when I woke up until I decided to try to sleep. From that perspective, it's hard not to think about what I did to cause this. How can it not be my fault? I couldn't care less about attention; I care about why and if I'm the reason for this. I want to be accountable for the pain I've caused. So, making it about me isn't something I'm trying to do. I just don't see how I can think about it in that way. All of these things are taking place for me every day. Not just his birthday, or the day he died, or when it's trendy to do so because it might get me some attention. Everything I just described was a hell that I dealt with every day during that first year.

As a thinker, I overthought just about everything at this time, so how people responded to me or just dealt with me, in general, made me feel some way, leading to me coming to conclusions about people. I developed an attitude that I care about that as much as you care about what I was going through. Again, I thought my way of thinking during this time made sense. Regardless of how rational it was or not. There are a lot of things that contributed to this way of thinking for me. The cliché phrases or the lack of understanding were the main ones, though. Phrases like "it will get better" or telling me things like everybody is going through something. Those were the types of things that were said to me during the first twelve months and beyond. The lack of understanding was shown in different ways, but the ones that shocked me the most were when I was written off as someone who just wanted to stay in the pain I was in simply because I didn't feel their methods of fixing me were for me at the time. It's weird because those people were also the same ones who will say everybody grieves differently. Later, it would turn into I'm just using my son's death as an excuse to do or not do what I want. That one is funny because those who may have felt that way also know me as an only child who did what I wanted to anyway, for the most part. I never needed an excuse to do what I wanted to do. These are some of the examples of things I was processing at the time.

I found myself asking people what exactly they were referring to when they said it would get better. Were they saying I would get better without a piece of me? That's the type of processing I was doing. I was trying to figure out why people didn't think before they said stuff like this. It hurt to think that no one could or would for one second just think of how they would want to be treated in a moment like that. Being in a place where you feel like no one understands what you're going through is the loneliest place in the world. To be a man in that place who came up under generations of men having the mentality that men should suffer whatever they are going through in silence. Until my son died, I guess I adopted that mentality as well, which is why I looked crazy, walking around looking, almost begging for someone to understand, care, or just comfort me. If I were about to think straight at the time, I would've realized that when it came to death, I've always been left alone to deal with the loss. From my Uncle James all the way down to my son, I've had to deal with death alone. That's probably why my attitude about death is the way it is, not realistic. Meaning I just didn't think about it, which meant it didn't affect me because it won't happen to people close to me. Losing my grandma hurt like hell, but because she was suffering, and that is more like the circle of life, I was able to accept it a lot sooner. I processed that on my own, but I learned as soon as my son died that I should've talked to someone about what I was feeling. I never learned how to process losing someone you love, but I was able to accept it because of the way I dealt with it. That's probably why I was able to accept death before losing my son. Again, my grandma's words kept ringing in my head, "You are not supposed to bury your child."

Being able to accept things in life, good or bad, is a very helpful tool to get through life; it has served me well thus far. The thing about that is the moment a loss happens that can't be explained, and it makes acceptance harder for me. That is exactly what happened when my son was taken from me. Because I couldn't come up with an explanation for such a random thing to happen. It made it harder for me to accept the fact that I'll never hug my son again. It kept those kind of thoughts front and center. Regardless of what I do or don't do, I constantly think that I won't see my son have a family of his own. All of those thoughts kept me in a place that has to be described as hell on earth. I could barely watch TV or listen to music without crying. Commercials, moves, hell, even sports on TV would make me cry. I had a problem with large groups of people, so I stayed to myself a lot.

I found myself driving aimlessly, sometimes in silence or with music for hours, or I would just go to the river and park there for hours. No matter what I did, though, I couldn't control the crying. I'm sure I cried more during the first six months than I have my entire life. It didn't matter when or where I saw something, heard something, or smelled something; it was all it would take for me to be in a full cry. Screaming, sobbing, cussing, and snotting were part of a daily routine for me. I didn't know what to do from one minute to the next. That pain of knowing I will never get that 'Happy Birthday Pops' call or text. I'd wake up every day and check my phone, hoping my son texted me, knowing he didn't. I also kept hoping that this wasn't real, that I would wake up and realize I was in a bad dream that I needed to learn from. Sometimes, almost eight years later, I find myself still hoping I will wake up and have a good long cry and then get a call from my son saying, "What's up, pop?" Thanks to my brother and the love I saw he and his father have for each other, being called pops by your son was like a badge of honor. I couldn't wait until the day I'd have a son call me pops. I wasn't sure what I had to do as a dad at the time to reach 'pop' status, but the moment I saw my son in the hospital, I realized that my love for him would make that happen, and again, I couldn't wait. That's why the moment he called me pops, I felt it was the moment I knew my son loved me. Being called pop was an achievement I will hold on to for the rest of my days.

In the midst of all of that, the only person I knew I had to worry about was my Babygirl. That itself was a separate hell for me simply because I know my baby felt cheated out of spending time with her brother while I was locked up, so when I got out, we were looking forward to our movie times together as well. To her credit, though, she never showed it. She talked to her dad no matter what, and we talked about all that we were both going through. We haven't discussed how she feels about missing that time with her brother due to my being locked up, but because I now have a baby girl, I know that may never be a conversation we have. Mainly because she knows I know these things, and I'm never going to say or act as though that's not why she missed that time. I just hope she also knows if she ever decides she wants to talk about that, I am more than willing to do so.

See, the thing about that, though, is that she, as well as her brother, could have had that resentment before he passed due to them Ghetto Twins! Sorry, that's funny! Being born in that situation was already a source of guilt for me, so I'm sure as they got older, it bothered them a little, or at the very least made them feel embarrassed at times. I know I did, which is why it was a constant source of guilt for me. It is a guilt that made me freeze up at times due to my not knowing what to do. It also is the guilt that led to my stupidity, which led to me being locked up. That being said, to their credit, they never showed whether or not either was an issue for them.

Although I have to say, knowing my daughter the way I do, I know it bothered her when he passed. She loved her brother, and not being able to have that relationship with him where they could build that bond as brother and sister bothered her and I am sure it does until this day. That's why it was insane for people to suggest that since she had younger siblings, she would be OK eventually. To be clear, when you ask if you have any other siblings, at that time being the first six months to a year, that's how it's going to come across to me and my daughter. Though she was her mom's only child for a while, she was never really an only child, so I wanted to make sure they knew each other. All of that contributed to the personal hell that not only I but my now only child were in. Tell me again how I'm not supposed to take that personally. Please, explain to me how I wanted to stay in that. It's easy to give a solution to a problem you don't understand, especially if you're not trying to understand the situation. It's also easy to dismiss a man as a lot of things when he's dealing with something that may require a real time out, which we all know for a man that's a no-no.

Again, as I said before, men suffer in silence, or at least are supposed to anyway. I never bought into that; I just never had that need or felt the need, until now, to talk to anyone. That was one thing I knew: I had to make sure my kids always knew they could talk to me no matter what. I thought it was important when I came home to make sure my son knew that. My baby has many women to talk to from different perspectives, and my input is valuable to her but it's an extra because she also has a lot of male relatives she rocks with. That was what I noticed when I came home. I could be that male voice for my son as well, just in different ways, but both ways are needed nonetheless.

These are all thoughts that are constantly repeated daily for me. Whether I want to think about it or not, whether I want to cry about it or not. I hate to sound repetitive, but it's important to emphasize how I was mentally and emotionally all over the place. I think that's important to know because if you saw me or dealt with me at that time, having an understanding of that may explain my actions or at least put them in perspective.

I started off writing this to explain to my loved ones where I was during that first year, starting November 28th, 2015. Not only did things I write about happen during that time, but I was also beginning to dig a hole for myself. I was hoping that giving a glimpse into where my mind was would lead to more understanding from those who are blessed enough not to have to go through something like this.

That's what it became as I started writing.

As hard as it still is to relive that time, it was a therapeutic thing to write these thoughts out. This is why it became even more important to stay within the time frame of the first twelve months after his death. That was the rawest time for me. It was the beginning of nothing ever being the same for me ever again in every way possible. This is why pushing the whole "back to normal" narrative is wild to me because my "normal" included someone who was no longer there, so how does that happen? I understand what the intent is in most cases where those sorts of statements are being said, but that does not take away from the way I heard it or took it.

The first year was the beginning of me seeing the world through different eyes, hearing with different ears, as well as thinking from a new perspective, and I had no idea all of that was happening at the time. From my perspective, I was able to see, hear, and think just fine. Unbeknown to me, the lack of me seeing that I was doing that, on top of the fact that no one knew to point it out to me. That created a disconnect between me and a lot of people who love me. Now, the biggest thing was during this time, it was hard for me to express myself, especially dealing with feelings I'd never dealt with before. Trying to articulate how I felt or what I needed was a true task, to say the least. It was hard to talk without emotion, which, for me, is exhausting. Before this, the only two people who could make me respond from a purely emotional place were my mom and my aunt TT. I hated it because I couldn't control it, and it always ended with me crying and then being mad because I was crying. As of 11/28/2015, EVERYBODY had that effect on me, and I couldn't turn it off.

Imagine being in a constant state of emotion where anything can send you over the edge. During my so-called normal times, I was basically on autopilot; if you asked me something, I could respond off of muscle memory sort of like a counterpuncher. When people talk to me, I can respond based on what they said, but I'm probably not there in the conversation. It was hard to care about things unrelated to me and my situation at the time, which is how I know that I have to make myself selfish because I felt bad for not caring what anyone else was going through at the time.

Especially having the attitude of, I care about what you're going through as much as you care about what I'm going through. Believe me, I know how that sounds, and that can be an unfair statement, but again, at the moment, that's just what it was. I also feel that if that statement makes you feel some type of way, I would suggest you look into how you handled my situation before you get upset about it. I also have to point out that one of my strong suits was patience. That is something that always served me well when dealing with kids. It's easy for me to have patience with kids of all ages because I didn't expect them to know better. Adults, on the other hand, are different.

I expect grown-ups to know better because they are older, but I realized how ridiculous that way of thinking was during this time. It didn't matter because having patience with anybody was not a thing for me. All of this emotion, confusion, anger, hurt, and lack of understanding made me sit in one spot for hours. It became harder to sleep, eat, or form a complete thought. There is an element of all over the place that I wanted to convey at the beginning of this book because I wanted to give a sense of where I was at that point. I was truly all over the place. If I don't accomplish anything else with this book, I truly hope that I can accurately describe where I was before losing my son as well as after. Knowing that you are going through something that no one wants to even consider a possibility makes the loneliness even louder. I couldn't articulate my feelings at the time because of the rawness of the emotions I was feeling. That, mixed with my lack of patience, had me spacing out at the drop of a dime, which, to someone who wants to help me, makes me look crazy.

Now, if I was not understanding or trying to understand what I was going through, it is easy to assume things about a person going through something like this. Things like, you don't want help, or you like the attention. I was using it as an excuse to do what I wanted. Then there's the ones that feel they have to say something for you to feel better, but it's really for them to be comfortable around you. That's when you get stuff like, "It will get better", which I know what the sentiment is behind that, but at the moment, that's not how it's taken. The explanation that it's supposed to get better without my child is insane to me, especially when a parent would say it. Knowing the person who says it, helps determine how I respond but it hurts every time it is said or implied. In that moment, all I can think of is how you did not know what you were saying or implying. How can you not know that at this moment, telling a parent to look forward to the future that doesn't include their child was not the best thing for me to hear? I understand that the reality of my situation is the rational way of taking that, but it's safe to say rational thinking went out the window on November 28th, 2015.

To be clear, I'm not telling anyone what to do or not do in

this situation. I do, however, feel that if I give those who are blessed enough never to have experienced something like this some insight as to what it feels like during the worst time in a parent's life. Before all that, everybody grieves differently; people chime in; yes, people do grieve differently.

Here's what I learned: it is true people deal with grief differently, but we all encounter the same symptoms. The difference is how we respond to those symptoms, especially when the variables are different.

Everyone's limits are different. Again, I understand all of that, but I also know how I truly felt in that moment and every day of my life since. What I think personally begins to come into play now because I can't keep my emotions in check.

You have to understand that I'm hearing differently, seeing differently, and thinking differently, and those differences were there to stay. I am forever changed due to the loss of my child. There is no getting back to normal. My normal included my son texting me or even calling me or me calling him. There is no better because my better requires my son to be here, and that's not happening. Again, I know how irrational that may sound, but I know from my perspective what it sounds like. At that moment, it was hard for me to care about anything but what my perspective was. I admit that at that moment, I was being severely selfish, so much so that when I would recognize it, I'd try to be different, but it never felt good to act as if, so that was just one more reason to stay to myself. Once again, this is another reason for the loneliness to get louder. Despite having multiple reasons for the lonely feeling, it still confused me at the time because I never had my son on a day-to-day basis. The more I thought about that, the more remarkable my son's mother became to me. Please understand that I had known, up until that point, that I have two of the best mothers of my kids I or any man could ask for. But when this happened, I thought about how if I had him every day of his life the way she did, I'm not sure I could have been as adult as she was every time I saw her. My other thought about his mom during the first twelve months was the fact that I may not have had the relationship I had with my son had she not been able to put her personal feelings aside and made our situation about our son.

A big part is that my kid's mother truly made it about the kids. My son's mom and I never really defined our situation, and my daughter's mom and I had been together since high school. Yeah, I know how that looks and sounds, and I never shied away from that, always taking full accountability for what I did. Which is a big part of the guilt I had before my son passed. That's something I've always felt shitty for. That being said, I have never, I repeat, *never* been to court for my kids or to see them. Due to their moms getting state aid of any kind, they had to put me on child support, which was the only thing that got me in front of a judge about my babies. They both had every right to be scorned women, but to their credit, they never did; as long as my kids loved me, they were good. My son's mom told me one day when I was dropping him off that as long as I kept showing I loved my son, I wouldn't have to worry about her trying to keep him from me. My baby girl's mom was the same way. She just didn't have to say it; as long as my baby loved me, she was good.

That, ladies and gentlemen, is what it looks like when you are doing it for the kids.

I'm sure some will read this and hear all my failures and say they were just accepting my mediocrity, and that's fine. They are allowed to feel that way. But I will ask them this: if they were different and hindered our relationship, how should I feel when something like this happens?

During the first twelve months after November 25th, 2015, the idea of how my relationship with my son could have been had his mom made our relationship about her personal feelings and not our sons. That is the blessing that I thought would run out on me, so I got stupid and ended up in prison. Despite all of that, I still came home to kids who wanted me around during their senior year. So call it what you want. At the end of the day, I had the relationship that I had with my son before he died because of his mom and later his stepdad. The stepdads, in this case, were also the best because they, too, could've also made it hard to maintain a relationship with my kids. Sadly, my situation with my kids and their moms is not the norm, so for a man to come into this situation and be OK with the dad not being dependable was, and I'm sure still is, at times, hard to do. To their credit, they adapted, and despite a few hiccups early, it has stayed the best situation for my babies. I hate to think about the hate and anger I would've been filled with during those first twelve months if his mom and stepdad were any other way. I can't begin to imagine how much worse off I would've been if I had to go through some of the things I've seen my friends go through in order to see their kids, let alone bond with them. That is why she became more of a marvel to me after we lost him, and she was able to be an adult in the times that required an adult because I was useless at the time. Unlike the popular opinion, it is very much possible to be in your kids' life as well as be great with the kids' mom without having to want to be with them. I've let her know this before in so many words, but I want to say that I will forever be grateful to my kids' moms and their stepdads for allowing the kids' feelings to take priority over theirs. That, to say the least, is why I will always be there for them however I can, whenever I can. I have a love for them that they will never understand.

November 28th, 2015, was the beginning of the worst year of my life as a parent, as well as a man. Some will say a loss is a loss if you cared for the person regardless of your relationship with the person you lost. The difference with the loss of a child, for me anyway, is the fact that it's not the natural order of things. It's not the circle of life. Like my grandma said, "You're not supposed to bury your child." The feeling from day to day after the 28th is something that I thought I would never feel in my life. It hurt in ways that have no words, and I couldn't eat, sleep, think, or hold a thought outside of the fact that I was never going to get a text from my son again. Weird as that may sound, I really couldn't get past that thought, especially the first ninety days. I'd wake up every day and check my phone for a text that was never coming. The few hours of sleep I got came from moments like this because I'd end up crying myself to sleep.

The crying was uncontrollable during those first twelve months, whether it was death-related or not. I couldn't watch TV or movies without crying and anything related to a parent's connection to their child. Didn't matter if it was father-son or how old the child was; the moment I realized they were connecting, I started crying. A lot of the time, I would end up driving for hours, stopping periodically to just sit in my car and listen to music or sit in silence. Yet another time and place for me to sit and cry uncontrollably as I realize just how fucked up this is. Every day was a struggle to even move, let alone be productive in any way. I did not fight for me. At that point, whatever happened to me just happened; from my perspective, what more could possibly be done to me? The fear of one day getting an answer to that question was paralyzing, knowing I would forever think of the moment I'd have to face that and not be able to handle it.

Having that feeling every day is what fed that need for comfort. Even if it was for a moment, I took it. I never expected anyone to know what to do or what to say, but I did, however, expect understanding. This goes a long way in this situation. I don't want my worst enemy to know what this feels like. I can't hate someone enough to wish this upon them. But to understand that all you can do is be there because I don't have a clue as to what I need. The only thing I wanted or needed at that time was my son. So, trying to make me think rationally at that time was useless. Trying to get me to see a bright side was pointless as well because, again, that bright side did not include my son. That was the only thing I wanted or needed at that time, especially during the first 90 days when I was checking my phone for a call or text.

Again, that's why understanding at that time was huge because, as irrational as I was, I knew no one could give me what I wanted at that time, or ever for that matter. If you can understand that, you are doing the best you can for a loved one who is going through this. Understand that this is not a fix-it situation, so you will not say or do something at that moment that will make that better, right, or easier. I feel sorry for those who've suffered this kind of loss and felt that tug or were encouraged to get back to normal or to have to live still. Those people have to act as if to get through the day, as well as make sure everyone is comfortable when you come around. The way I'm wired wouldn't allow me to act as if, not to mention that's how I got through prison for the most part and the fact that I couldn't care less about people's comfort around me at that time. I paid no attention to that part at all. I, too, have to be understanding as well when it comes to people and the way they deal with me. I had to understand that depending on who was saying or doing something that was viewed as pointless, the intent was something I had to pay attention to. That was very important. Because what no one knew or could've known at that time, including me, was that the way people dealt with me during that time affected our relationship. Regardless of the relationship, the effect was different, not necessarily bad or good, just different due to my withdrawal from people, period. My being distant from everyone didn't come across as a change in any of my relationships. That's where understanding me comes into play, and again, I was slow, but depending on the relationship I had with the person, I did feel I had to be rational at some point. Whenever I felt someone didn't understand that I felt should, I knew I had to try to be as rational as I could be at the time. This was hard because all I wanted at that time were things that weren't rational, so the majority of my thoughts were off and irrational, to say the least.

Keep in mind that this is the first twelve months after God decided to pick my life up by the ankles and shake it while turning it upside down. It felt as if the world sped up and left me where I was. I could see the world moving as I sat in one place and didn't care, not one bit. See, as I'm watching the world continue without giving a damn about what just happened to my baby, I began to change. I did not fully realize it at that time, but I began to get more selfish when it came to my mental as well as my feelings, which is what fed the mentality of I care about that as much as you cared about what I'm going through. At that time, I was blissfully OK with it. Fairness wasn't part of the equation at that time, which is also why I knew and felt selfishness. As an only child, I got accused of being selfish, and it fits at times about certain things. But in general, I never felt like a truly selfish person until the worst time in my life happened.

As bad as that sounds and felt at times, I, at the time, was 100% fine with it. Looking back, I can give you a lot of great explanations for my mindset during that time, but at that moment, I couldn't. Not only that, but I couldn't even tell you if what I was doing was right or not. But what I knew was it felt good to do. All of my emotional responses to whatever set me off were raw and genuine and felt good to get out, and since I didn't have a lot of control over my emotions at the time, nor did I know what would set me off, those emotional responses were coming fast and hot. Please don't mistake my not caring for enjoyment or taking any pleasure in having the mentality that I was acquiring, but knowing it wasn't a productive mentality, and I also knew how I felt in the moment. It was because of that feeling I truly knew I didn't care. From my perspective, why should I? If I was bad enough to take my son while I was trying to care, why should I care at all now?

Yes, irrational thinking at its finest. I started this glimpse into the worst year of a parent's life by explaining a lot of things that were happening to me at the time. The biggest first was losing a child and instantly becoming a different person. An even bigger first was the emotional reaction to everything. Going from a person who thought before reacting to someone who just reacts absent of any thought is exhausting. It is draining and not conducive to maintaining employment, especially if you work in factories. From my perspective, for me to work in factories as I did up until that point, I had to be able to look over and flat-out ignore being treated a certain way regardless of what kind of factory it was. At the end of the day, I always understood they don't have to care about anything but their product and bottom line. Well, as of November 28th, 2015, that understanding no longer exists for me, so every time I heard, felt, or experienced their lack of care, I'd responded. Needless to say, that never ended well for me, especially since I was probably in the wrong in the first place. Regardless of how much I needed a job, I didn't care. The moment I felt they didn't, it usually was my last day.

The other firsts for me were small but impactful, nonetheless. All of these firsts that take place after the worst time in my life as a parent will forever be present in who I will be for the rest of my life. The problem with that is I had no clue that was happening, so from my perspective, I wasn't changing. No one was understanding or caring about what I was going through. Like I said before, understanding was the only thing I was expecting, which is why I gravitated towards that regardless of where it came from. If I felt the stranger I was talking to understood what I was going through, I'd talk to them as long as they'd allow me. I feel as though I have to reiterate that my being selfish during this time was a direct result of my irrational way of thinking at the time, even though I had to be selfish in that moment since my sanity was my responsibility with guilt and lack of confidence leading the way during the worst year of my life in its entirety.

Realizing how much I failed before this happened helps me keep what's happening in perspective. Failing at life due to my own bad decisions was an acceptable pill to swallow, especially since I could learn from them. The way I'm wired makes it easier for me to accept things when I can learn and do better from a failure. The problem for me with failing to protect my child was I couldn't accept that which meant I couldn't move past him being gone. Which also meant I couldn't learn anything from this. In the midst of this, I truly couldn't see that ever getting any better, which further led to my all-over-the-place behavior. The thought that maybe this wouldn't hurt so much if I were a better parent lived rent-free in my mind, especially since I knew, or at least felt like I knew, just how much of a failure I'd been. Now, I get that whole argument that as long as I think like that, I will forever stay in that state that I was in. My response to that is always the same, which is I can't act like those thoughts and feelings don't exist. The type of person I am naturally, I have to process all the variables of the situation, especially if it involves my feelings. I have to acknowledge those emotions to get through them, acting as if it just does not work for me. I have to go through to get through, and I promise you nothing about that says I want to stay in that state. That, for me, is my process of going through emotional things, and in this situation where no one knows what to do, I have to deal with every emotion.

I never understood how people could go through emotional things and not acknowledge all the different emotions that come with whatever the situation. By no means am I saying that everyone who loses a child feels and acts the way I did, but I'm sure a version of all those thoughts and feelings crossed their minds. How it affects you and the amount of time it affects you is different, but I don't believe all those emotions are felt. I applaud those who can do that, and it genuinely works. I would never attempt to write a book trying to advise on what to do in this situation because, at the end of the day, I truly know you have to go through this to figure it out. However, I feel like I can help those close to the ones who have lost a child better understand how to be there or not be there if they're not capable. I can't express how important that understanding is during the first year of this happening. For a man, let alone a black man, having someone understand you is something that you cherish and certainly don't take lightly, and that was before the tragedy. After losing my son, I realized no one understands or is trying to understand, so when I feel or see someone understanding or trying to understand, I naturally gravitate to them.

Thankfully, I was blessed to have a few expected and unexpected people in my life who offered that understanding. Even with those people in my life, I still found myself feeling alone. See, that's what I want also to make clear: even if you have someone there to give you the understanding and comfort you need, you will still be going through alone it. I hate that I even felt necessary to write something like this. The reason it was needed and the fact that I can write about it says a lot about the unpredictability this whole thing causes. From one minute to the next, from one day to the next, I had no clue what to do. The awkwardness I felt around people from simply not knowing how to talk to people without going into what I was going through was a lot, at times, too much. To say I was in my head a lot would be an understatement. I was always worried about my presence changing the mood of any room I walked into.

I worried about how long before people got tired of me processing what I was dealing with, would people even deal with me before it became too much for them to want to deal with. I worried, but I didn't care, and I was constantly in thought about all of this. Imagine having all of these things going on in your head while knowing and feeling like the only thing that can make those thoughts and fears go away was the return of my son and waiting for that to happen. It was to the point of me not accepting his death or anything related to his death or the acceptance of his death.

I was not too far removed from learning how much acceptance can make moving through things in life a little easier no matter how fucked up. Thanks to prison and the place where I needed that mentality the most, I refused to think that way. I never saw my son's casket go in the ground, so it helped me not accept it, not to mention I just didn't want to. Lack of acceptance, lack of confidence, no motivation, fear, guilt, anger, confusion, loneliness, and the inability to control any of these or any other emotion I had. That, in a nutshell, was the worst year of my life, summed up in words. My reason for focusing on the first year only with the book is because this is the beginning of me becoming a different person. Yes, some, if not most, of the core parts of who I am as a man, parent, friend, and family member are still there, but they have all been affected in some way, shape, or form. I feel like giving the world an eye-opening understanding that I'll help in the healing process for others who, unfortunately, are dealing with a loss like this. Again, I never want anyone to know what this feels like, but I do think having an understanding of what that person is feeling going through allows you to help one person from saying, "It will get better" because they now understand, then I fee my writing hit its mark.

In all seriousness, I feel like understanding is very low across the board in today's world, or it's loaded as a form of acceptance. Please be clear this is not a book to expose bad behavior. It is, however, a book explaining as well as acknowledging my behavior. I feel it needs to be said that understanding does not mean acceptance. Understanding someone's position on something or why they did it doesn't change the act, but it puts it in perspective. That's not accepting the act at all but it can be the difference in how you deal with that person from now on. That's why understanding is so important in this situation, or at least it was to me. That's also why those who gave that understanding, or at least from my perspective, will forever have a special place with me regardless of what our relationship was prior. As a black man, having someone give the impression of understanding, or dare I say, actually care about what I'm doing, is a feeling that can't be put into words. That feeling can make a man feel like he can do anything, from something as big as becoming the president of the United States to as small as feeling like you are not alone at that worst time in your life. Understanding is very powerful when used more than judgment. Unfortunately, for men, when we go through things that affect our mental, there is a lot less tolerance or understanding. Especially if it affects their life in any way, that's when the judgment comes into play, along with the impatience of dealing with a man whose mind requires care, comfort, or a little concern.